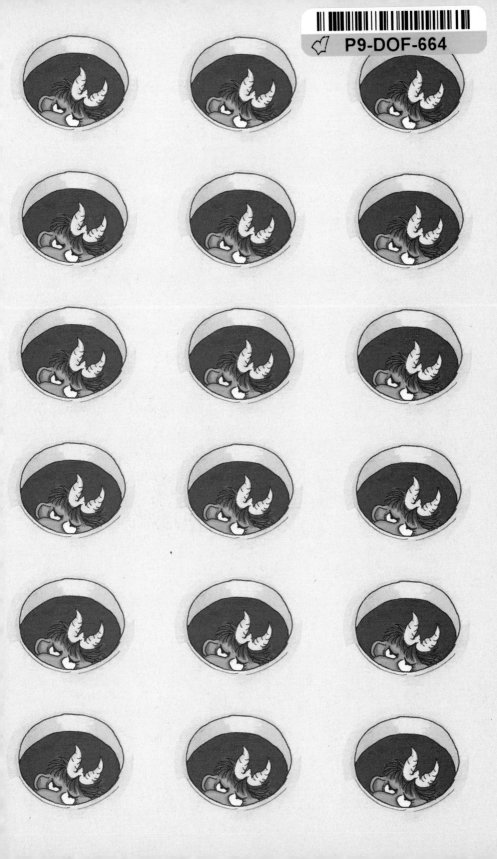

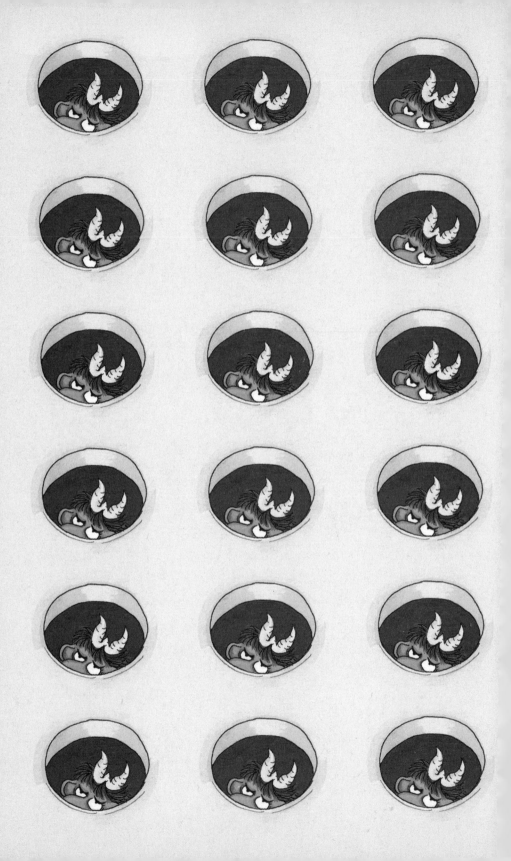

OF RELATED INTEREST

OUTSMARTING WORRY

AN OLDER KID'S GUIDE TO MANAGING ANXIETY

DAWN HUEBNER, PhD

ILLUSTRATED BY KARA McHALE

Jessica Kingsley *Publishers*
London and Philadelphia

First published in 2018
by Jessica Kingsley Publishers
73 Collier Street
London N1 9BE, UK
and
400 Market Street, Suite 400
Philadelphia, PA 19106, USA
www.jkp.com

Library of Congress Cataloging in Publication Data
A CIP catalog record for this book is available from
the Library of Congress

British Library Cataloguing in Publication Data
A CIP catalogue record for this book is available from the British Library

ISBN 978 1 78592 782 9
eISBN 978 1 78450 702 2

Printed and bound in the United States

Contents

Introduction to Readers

NERVOUS UNEASY
AGITATED Upset
JITTERY PERTURBED
SCARED EDGY
Fretful STRESSED

It doesn't matter if you use fancy words, or simple ones. We all worry. Not just the people who pick up this book, but everyone.

Sometimes worry serves a useful purpose, directing our attention to actual threats. Things we need to pay attention to, or prepare for.

Sometimes worry isn't helpful, like when we fret over something we don't have control over, or can't predict. But even this kind of worry doesn't cause too much trouble as long as we go about our business, and let the feeling fade away.

Then there's a third kind of worry. The kind that gets in the way. Worry – with an upper-case W. A greedy monster. Out to cause trouble. This kind of Worry makes easy things seem hard, and hard things impossible. It gets too big, too fast.

Upper-case Worry keeps you from doing things that are fun and important. Things that are safe. This kind of Worry can seriously interfere with your life.

Unfortunately, Worry is a clever creature. It uses tricks to fool you, tricks designed to lure you deeper into its clutches. But upper-case Worry is also predictable. And for every one of its tricks, there's a way to outsmart it.

And the best thing is, it doesn't matter what you are worried about – bees or making mistakes or being laughed at or the dark – the same outsmarting techniques will work for any fear.

It's like math. There is a set of basic operations. You learn them, and then it doesn't matter what the numbers are. You just plug your numbers into the operations you've learned, and the problem will be solved.

Same here.

You'll learn how worry (lower-case) turns into Worry (upper-case), and the tricks this Worry plays. And then you will learn the operations. How to fight back. How to plug in your concerns, whatever they might be, so you can outsmart Worry, no matter what form it is taking.

Read the Note to Parents and Caregivers on the next page if you want more information, or skip right to Chapter 1 and get started.

A Note to Parents and Caregivers

Everyone worries from time to time. Anxiety is a normal human feeling. Helpful, even, when it motivates us to solve problems and take productive action. But a normal level of anxiety about realistic concerns is not what this book is about.

Outsmarting Worry is geared toward 9–13-year-olds struggling with unrealistic fears, children who shrink away from normal challenges and fret about unlikely scenarios. It is intended for children who quickly shift from worry (lower-case) to Worry (upper-case). Who can't seem to move away from their fearful imaginings.

Sometimes unrealistic worries crop up unexpectedly. Other times they are triggered by a clear and specific stressor. Either way, upper-case Worry is often part of a pattern, a way of thinking and being in the world. It gets ingrained, like a habit. Without intervention, Worry can become a way of life.

Whether it's about one thing or many, Worry gets in the way, making sleep and school and family life difficult. It quickly takes over. If this sort of Worry is significantly interfering with your child's life, please talk to your doctor or seek help from a mental health professional.

While this book cannot take the place of therapy, it can introduce you and your child to a set of skills including strategies based on Cognitive Behavioral Therapy (CBT) and techniques arising from Acceptance and Commitment

Therapy (ACT). These skills – when practiced diligently – have proven remarkably effective in the treatment of anxiety. And the good news is, it doesn't matter what your child is worried about – bad grades, making mistakes, new experiences, storms, vampires, bees, vomiting, dying – the same set of skills applies.

Whether your child's difficulties are longstanding or new, and whether you are working with a therapist or on your own, your child will benefit most if you read this book together. Discuss the content. Help your child substitute their own worries for those described in the examples. Actively talk about the feelings your child is struggling with, following the guidelines to create self-talk and practice activities relevant to your child's fears.

Then work with your child to translate newfound knowledge into action. You will learn, for example, that looking for evidence of feared outcomes is important, and that doing something makes it less scary. But knowing these things is not enough. Until your child practices the techniques in this book, their fear will remain locked in place.

Be patient and persistent. You are your child's best coach and guide. Together you can change, moving from learning to practicing, from worried to happy and free.

Starting is easy. Simply turn the page, and begin.

CHAPTER 1

Getting Started

They all mean the same thing: a person with special knowledge and abilities.

Being a person with special knowledge and abilities doesn't happen by magic *.★

It takes reading and studying, listening and experimenting. Expertise takes work. Lots of work. You have to learn and practice – know and do – over and over again.

Almost everyone has expertise in something. Maybe you are an expert skate-boarder, or gymnast, or guitar player. Some children are expert gamers. Others can list dinosaurs by diet, sink balls into baskets, flip pancakes, add fractions, dance hip hop. Perhaps you have expertise in history, weather patterns, sports statistics, fashion trends.

None of this expertise happened by accident. It took learning and practicing. Knowing and doing. Again. And again. And again.

Chances are good you are reading this book because you are an expert at worrying.

Unfortunately, it's easy to become an expert at worrying. You worry about bad things happening. You try to avoid those bad things, and you get people to reassure you about them. But you can't control whether (or not) bad things happen, and it occurs to you that the reassurances might be wrong. So, you worry more. And more. And soon you can't stop worrying, which gives you all the practice you need to become an expert at worrying.

But listen to this. Lean down close to the page so you don't miss a thing because this next sentence just might change your life. You can go from being an expert at worrying to an expert at managing worry. You can learn everything you need to know, do everything you need to do, to outsmart your worries. It's true. Thousands of children have done it, and you can too.

Are you ready to begin?

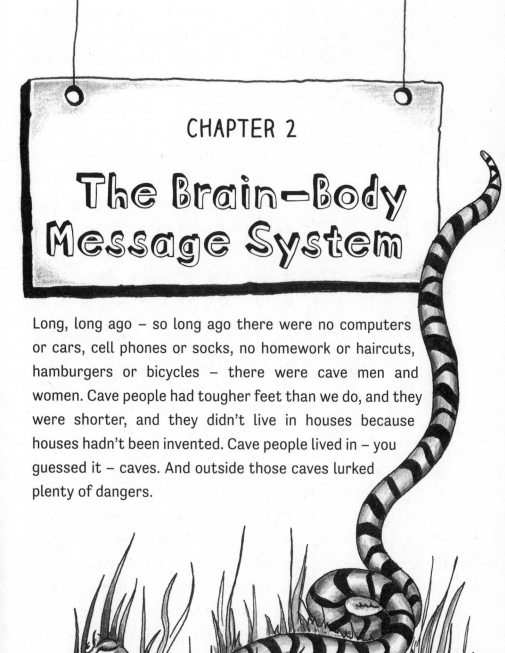

CHAPTER 2

The Brain–Body Message System

Long, long ago – so long ago there were no computers or cars, cell phones or socks, no homework or haircuts, hamburgers or bicycles – there were cave men and women. Cave people had tougher feet than we do, and they were shorter, and they didn't live in houses because houses hadn't been invented. Cave people lived in – you guessed it – caves. And outside those caves lurked plenty of dangers.

There were woolly mammoths and snakes, scorpions and saber-toothed tigers, earthquakes and volcanoes and storms. And because cave people didn't have meteorologists or smoke detectors or police departments or cages, they had to be very, very careful. Anything could slither up, bubble up, rumble up, or pop up. Anything could happen in the blink of an eye.

Cave people had to be clever if they wanted to stay alive. They had to stay alert. Be aware of the snap of a twig. A darkening sky. A smell on the breeze. All could mean danger.

So, cave people's brains changed over time, getting better and better at noticing potential dangers. Their bodies changed, too, allowing them to spring into action at the first sign of trouble. That's a good thing. If a saber-toothed tiger pounced, it would be ridiculous to carefully consider every option. It would be smarter to react – and fast!

Cave people developed a speedy message system between their brains and bodies, a message system designed to react quickly to increase the chance of survival.

As soon as a tiny part in the cave person's brain – a part called the amygdala (ah-MIG-duh-la) – detected DANGER, it triggered a surge of chemicals that prepared the cave person for action. Muscles tightened. Hearts speeded up. Blood raced through arteries towards arms and legs, giving them energy to swing a large stick or run. Stomachs slowed down because the work of digesting food was less important than the work of fighting or running away.

This whole cascade of changes is called the "fight-or-flight response" (flight as in flee, scram, make haste, clear the decks, vamoose, RUN), and it's one of the things that kept cave people alive.

The fight-or-flight response keeps us alive, too.

You see, our brains and bodies are like those of our cave people ancestors: not so hairy, but still designed to immediately recognize danger and protect us.

Three cheers for the amygdala!

GO AMYGDALA

CHAPTER 3

Danger Learning and Safety Behaviors

When something scary happens, or when you hear something scary that might happen, your amygdala sets off an alarm triggering the fight-or-flight response. Your body gets super-charged, and your brain takes an instant picture.

Whatever you are hearing and seeing and smelling and feeling gets captured under the heading: Danger. That way, when you hear or see or smell or feel those things in the future, you will know to be afraid – and be careful – because those sounds, sights, smells, etc. were associated with danger in the past. This is called Danger Learning, and our brains are really good at it.

Keep in mind that the amygdala is on the lookout for anything that might hurt us. Not just physical pain, but also embarrassment, or emotional upset of any kind. If you feel completely in the dark about what your History teacher is expecting on a big project, or if you are standing at a counter, waiting to order your own food for the first time – your amygdala might call: Alert! Alert! Basically, we don't like feeling unsure of ourselves or uncomfortable in any way, so lots of things get interpreted as DANGER.

Danger Learning happens quickly, and is followed by vigorous attempts to stay safe. Again, this makes total sense.

We want to stay alive, both now and in the future, so we do what we need to do to keep ourselves safe. If whatever we do works – we're safe! we're alive! – we know to do those things each time we encounter The Danger.

A one-time encounter with a bad thing is enough to set this off. That makes sense. It would be silly to have to get bitten by a saber-toothed tiger three times before deciding that running away was the right strategy.

So, experiencing a bad thing – or even thinking a bad thing might happen – gets you thinking about taking precautions. Thinking about what you need to do, before the bad thing even happens, to keep yourself safe.

Let's say your brother burns his mouth on hot soup. Chances are good you'll decide to blow on your soup before slurping it down.

Or if you feel tongue-tied talking to someone you like (you know, really like), you will probably find yourself feeling hesitant to talk to them in the future, in case it happens again.

Blowing on hot soup, being shy around your new crush – these are things you do to stay safe. To protect yourself from real (or imagined – we'll get to that part later) dangers.

Because they are behaviors, and because they are designed to keep you safe, these actions are called – drumroll, please –

SAFETY BEHAVIORS.

Safety Behaviors are the things you do, the specific actions you take, to stay safe. Physically or emotionally. Now and in the future.

When used in truly dangerous situations, Safety Behaviors are helpful. They protect you. Make bad things less likely to happen.

Wearing a helmet (a Safety Behavior) makes you less likely to get hurt when you are riding your bicycle. Brushing your teeth and flossing (both Safety Behaviors) make you less likely to get cavities. Most Safety Behaviors are healthy, and make sense.

When we perform Safety Behaviors, we feel better, too. We study our spelling words and feel more confident going into the test. We carry a cell phone, and feel better about going out alone.

So, there is a two-for-one benefit with Safety Behaviors: we increase the chances of staying safe, and we don't feel so afraid.

What an ingenious system.

Except sometimes, it goes horribly wrong.

CHAPTER 4

False Alarms

When things are going as they should, your amygdala sounds the alarm about real dangers. Your fight-or-flight response gets triggered and you do what you need to do to protect yourself, both now and in the future.

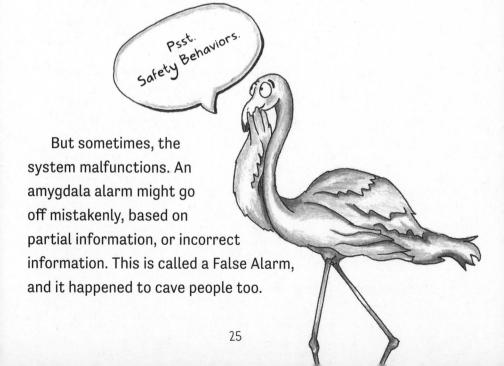

Psst.
Safety Behaviors.

But sometimes, the system malfunctions. An amygdala alarm might go off mistakenly, based on partial information, or incorrect information. This is called a False Alarm, and it happened to cave people too.

SCENARIO: A cave person might be strolling along enjoying the sunshine, or watching a butterfly flit among the flowers. The grass nearby rustles and – whoosh – the cave person is filled with heart-pounding, muscle-tightening, stick-grabbing, legs-ready energy.

Except sometimes the rustling of grass is only a breeze. Or a jackrabbit (a tasty meal totally destroyed if the cave person were to pummel it 20 times). The rustling might be a harmless snake. Or a friend who hadn't been around for days. It would hardly do to club the cave-friend, or even that harmless snake. Both would be a waste of energy, and might make the cave person feel foolish afterwards.

So, cave people had to learn to tell the difference between real dangers and False Alarms. To know that not every bend in the grass is a woolly mammoth. Otherwise, they would always assume the worst, and spend far too much time clubbing grass and running away from nothing at all.

It's like that with us, too. We modern-day humans need to learn the difference between real dangers and False Alarms. Mistaking one for the other causes all sorts of trouble, and makes us feel needlessly afraid.

The most common cause of amygdala False Alarms is Worry.

Imagine Worry – Worry with an upper-case W – as something separate from you. A little creature. A monster, or critter, or pest. It acts like a friend – there to protect and keep you safe – but really Worry's aim is to frighten you.

Worry is like that annoying classmate. You know the one. The person who plops down next to you, then jumps up and shouts:

There's a spider on your leg!

Spider?! Your amygdala would pull the alarm, sending a jolt of energy through your body. You'd jump up, and immediately start brushing your leg. Ick!

But wait. Even though you're in fight-or-flight mode and your heart is pounding, your brain would begin to register: I didn't see any spider.

A minute or two later, your classmate does it again:

There's a spider on your leg!

You'd probably startle again. Amygdala alarm! Although not quite as intense. You'd stay seated this time, but your heart would still be pounding and you'd still look down. Is there a spider?

No. No sign of a spider.

You'd throw a puzzled glance at your classmate.

And then, again:

> There's a spider on your leg!
> There's a spider on your leg!

Now it's getting downright annoying.

> There's a spider on your leg!
> There's a spider on your leg!

How many times would it take for your amygdala to stop going off, and for you to stop reacting entirely? Three times, maybe four?

You might get a little blip of fear each time you hear "Spider!" – that's just your amygdala taking some time to catch up – but mostly you'd feel puzzled and annoyed, as well you should.

Your classmate has proven himself to be an unreliable source of information. You'd catch on to that quickly, and stop jumping. Eventually you'd say, "Look, cut it out" or you'd open your book and tune him out entirely. That would be the right thing to do.

Which brings us back to Worry. Worry is like that annoying classmate. It sounds an alarm:

> You're going to get sick!

> You're going to mess up!

> You're going to be alone!

> Everyone will laugh at you!

> Something terrible will happen!

Often the same alarm, over and over.

And now you know: There is no need to jump.

Worry is an unreliable source of information. It pulls your amygdala alarm, saying something that sounds scary – that would be scary – if it was true. But it's a False Alarm. There's no evidence that what your Worry is saying is true.

Evidence. That turns out to be important. In fact, it's the first key to outsmarting Worry.

CHAPTER 5

Where's the Evidence?

Worry is a trickster. It says things designed to trigger your amygdala. Things that sound scary – that would be scary – except for one small detail. There are no facts supporting them.

Let's go back to our early ancestors, the cave people, to learn more about the importance of evidence.

SCENARIO: Pretend someone told a cave woman about a bear they once spotted near a swamp known for its juicy berries. Bears were all around back then, and it absolutely made sense to be afraid of them.

The cave woman might have headed to the swamp anyway, her love of berries and knowledge that others had been to the swamp without problems outweighing her fear. But as she gets closer, her Worry decides to play a trick and whispers, *"Bear!"*

The cave woman's heart starts pounding. Her muscles get tight. She begins to feel panicky, even though she doesn't see or hear or smell a bear. But still, "Bear!" says her Worry. "AAAAAAAAH" says her amygdala. And she begins to run, deciding she isn't hungry for berries after all.

The cave woman listened to her Worry and left the swamp, but she shouldn't have. There wasn't enough evidence of danger. Evidence is proof. Not what *might be* or *could be* but what *is*.

We modern-day people make this mistake, too.

My dad is late. what if something bad happened?

It's raining hard! what if my house gets hit by lightning?

One tiny possibility, but your Worry pulls an amygdala alarm – Alert! Alert! Alert! – and it becomes the thing you focus on, and dread, and suddenly have to go to great lengths to avoid.

Maybe. Might be. Could be. All about dire possibilities.

How can you recognize these tricks, and outsmart Worry?

By following your nose.

Well...not exactly. Not the kind of nose on your face (although you do spend a great deal of time following that one). You need to follow the other kind of nose: your *Knows*.

Your "Knows" are the things you know for sure. Not the things Worry tells you *might* happen. Not the things Worry reminds you *can* happen. Not the things you once heard and now dread, or want desperately to avoid. Your Knows are the things you have proof of. The things that evidence tells you are true.

Psst. Your Knows.

When Worry rears its ugly head (and pulls your amygdala alarm), ask yourself, "Do I know that terrible thing is going to happen?" You will find the answer is almost always, "I don't know. At least not for sure." That's because Worries aren't about knowing, they are about thinking (or feeling) that something is true, often despite tons of evidence to the contrary.

OUTSMARTING TECHNIQUE

When you find yourself worrying about something, your first question should always be, "where's the evidence?"

worry: That dog is going to bite you.
child: Where's the evidence?

worry: You're going to get sick.
child: Where's the evidence?

worry: You are going to mess up.
child: Where's the evidence?

You get the idea.
   Then, look for evidence.

worry: That dog is going to bite you.

child: The dog is just standing
         there. Other people are
         walking by and it isn't
         growling or snarling or
         opening its mouth at all.
         The dog is wagging its
         tail, which means it's happy.
         There is no evidence
         that it wants
         to bite me,
         or anyone.

34

Your Worry wants you to think, *all dogs are dangerous!* and the risk of a bite is huge. But that's not what the evidence shows. People are around dogs all the time. The risk is miniscule (really, really small). And that dog, in particular, isn't showing any signs of danger.

Good job! You followed your Knows, and are on your way to outsmarting Worry.

Except wait. What's that?

A little Worry voice, "It's true, the dog's just standing there now. But it might see you AND BITE YOU."

Don't fall for it.

That's Worry's version of "There's a spider on your leg!" Sounds scary, but no evidence that it's true. Keep following your Knows. And read on.

CHAPTER 6
Thinking Mistakes

Worry tries to scare you – and often succeeds – because when it pulls the alarm, it *feels* like you really are in danger.

Remember, the danger feeling comes from your amygdala, and the fight-or-flight response, which gets set off even for False Alarms.

And even for False Alarms, that danger feeling will linger. That's because it takes time – often 15 or 20 minutes – for the fight-or-flight response to settle down. Unfortunately, during that time, Worry will be hard at work.

The fight-or-flight response makes thinking hard. Blood is rushing away from your brain towards your arms and legs (getting them ready to fight or run), and you are focused on staying safe, not on looking for evidence.

Worry takes advantage of that. It whispers additional scary thoughts, to magnify the initial alarm.

Fortunately, Worry isn't very creative. It tries to scare you using Thinking Mistakes. The same mistakes, over and over again.

A Thinking Mistake is a Worry Trick designed to keep you scared.

You can learn to catch Worry, especially once you know the most common Thinking Mistakes it uses.

Here are three:

Thinking Mistake #1: Exaggerating Likelihood
The thing you are afraid of IS going to happen. Definitely. For sure.

Thinking Mistake #2: Catastrophic Thinking
It will be the worst thing you can possibly imagine. A super-horrible full-blown all-out disaster.

Thinking Mistake #3: You Can't Handle It
This is so much worse than anything you've ever dealt with. Forget about even trying.

Of course, the outsmarting strategy for Thinking Mistakes is to recognize them, and correct them. You'll be better able to do that if you read a bit more about each.

Thinking Mistake #1: Exaggerating Likelihood
The thing you fear IS going to happen. Just because something MIGHT happen doesn't mean it WILL happen. Ask yourself, "where's the evidence?" Pay attention to what is actually, factually true. And if there are no facts, go with what is most likely.

Getting hit by lightning? Extremely unlikely. How do you know? Well, does the rest of your family dive for cover when the sky turns gray? Have you or anyone you know been hit by lightning any of the hundreds of times you have been out in the rain? Do you even see lightning most times when it rains?

Sure it's possible for there to be lightning, but getting hit is really, really rare. Thinking the bad thing IS going to happen, that's just a Worry Trick.

Thinking Mistake #2: Catastrophic Thinking

It will be the worst thing you can possibly imagine. Worries take little bad things and turn them into BIG bad things. Terrible things. Catastrophes.

Let's say your dad is late picking you up. That's a little bad thing. But Worry wants it to seem like a big bad thing. Instead of remembering all the normal reasons people run late, your Worry might scream, "He was in an accident! He's lying in a ditch!"

What are the more likely possibilities for your father running late? He probably got stuck in traffic. Or got a call at the last minute. Or maybe even stopped to buy toppings for homemade pizza.

So, yes, little bad things do sometimes happen (your dad might be late) but catastrophes are really rare.

Thinking Mistake #3: You Can't Handle It

This is so much worse than anything you've ever dealt with. Forget about even trying. Worries have a way of making you forget that you are a competent person. Competent means you can solve problems and deal with tough situations.

Your Worry wants you to think your dad's being late is a catastrophe. But chances are good he's late for a frustrating-but-silly reason, an ordinary reason, and he'll arrive soon. In the meantime, you can talk to a friend or read a book or listen to music. There are plenty of ways to pass the time while waiting for your dad.

And even if something bad has happened – which is unlikely – there are still things you can do, people you can turn to, ways you can cope. Your Worry doesn't want you to know that, but it's true.

So, two steps.

First, you **identify** the Thinking Mistake. Then you **correct it**.

Here's what that looks like:

Worry: Your stomach hurts. You're going to get sick!

child: That's Mistake #1: Exaggerating Likelihood. My stomach feels this way a lot, and I rarely throw up. When I get busy my stomachache goes away.

Worry: Don't raise your hand! What if you're wrong?! The teacher is going to get mad, and everyone will laugh.

child: That's Mistake #1: Exaggerating Likelihood and Mistake #2: Catastrophic Thinking. I do know the answer and even if I'm wrong, my teacher will help me figure out the right answer. No one laughs when other kids are wrong, and they won't laugh at me, either.

Worry:	No one is going to sit with you on the bus! You'll be alone, and everyone will be staring, and it will be horrible!
child:	Nice try, Worry, but that's all three Thinking Mistakes! It's true that sometimes there's an awkward moment when I first get on the bus. But I know lots of people, and I usually find someone to sit with, and even if I don't, I can read or listen to music.

With practice, it's easy to see Thinking Mistakes for what they are: Worry at work. Overblown fears about bad things that are unlikely to happen. Exaggerated fears about how awful things will be, and how incompetent you are.

But you're not incompetent. You are a clever person able to solve problems and cope. You can outsmart this Worry Trick. You can identify Thinking Mistakes, and correct them. The more you practice, the easier it will get.

And remember:

You CAN'T trust a Worry.

CHAPTER 7

Worry Loves to Debate

To outsmart Worry, you have to recognize the tricks it is using to ensnare you, tricks like setting off False Alarms, and planting Thinking Mistakes. You can respond to these tricks by recognizing what is happening, and talking back.

Talking back to Worry is a great strategy, but be careful. Worry loves nothing more than a good debate. You know, the kind that goes on and on. And that Worry ultimately wins.

Worries are tenacious. That means they don't give up.

You might be tenacious, too. Usually that's a good thing, to not give up, but endlessly arguing with Worry is useless.

For one thing, it's a waste of time. A you-versus-Worry debate will go on and on with no satisfying resolution.

And for another, Worry has a powerful card up its sleeve. A simple question designed to stop you cold:

WORRY TRICK

Are you sure?

Ugh.

Because as soon as Worry asks, you realize the answer is "No." You're not sure. Whatever you are worried about, you can't be sure it is (or isn't) going to happen. And then it seems – because you're not sure – that Worry must be right. You're doomed.

That's how Worry wins.

Or tries to win.

Or used to win.

But not anymore, because you can outsmart this Worry Trick, too. You can Talk Back without debating, and without falling into Worry's "Are you sure?" trap.

OUTSMARTING TECHNIQUE

Keep in mind that no one has a crystal ball. Not you. Not your parents. Not your teachers, or your therapist, or your friends.

PSST. NEITHER DOES WORRY.

NICE TRY WORRY

That means that no one knows what the future holds. Everyone lives with uncertainty. All the time. Even you.

Usually, it's not a big deal.

When you walk into a room, you don't know for sure that you aren't going to stub your toe. But you walk into rooms anyway, without cowering away from furniture.

You don't know for sure that you aren't going to catch your hand in a car door, or burp loudly at lunchtime, or fall out of bed. But you slam car doors and munch down tuna sandwiches and climb into bed anyway. You take chances all the time. We all do.

So when Worry asks, "Are you sure?" don't fall into the trap of thinking you need to be sure. Recognize this as a silly question. A Worry Trick. Of course you aren't sure. No one is.

 Outsmart Worry by saying, "Nope, I'm not sure. But that's okay."

Because it is okay. It has to be. Uncertainty is part of everyone's life.

Let's think about what this looks like. Both the debating part, and how to handle Worry's "Are you sure?"

Pretend Worry is bothering you about getting sick, making you think you could get sick, you WILL get sick, and that it will be awful.

It seems like Worry is right. It would be awful. Getting sick is really uncomfortable, and embarrassing (if you're at school), and scary.

But you remember what you've been reading, and decide to try talking back.

Worry: What if you get sick?

child: I'm not going to get sick!

worry: How do you know?

child: I don't have a fever.

worry: But your stomach hurts.

child: That's because you're bothering me!

worry: Really? Once your stomach felt this way, and you did get sick.

child: Well, I'm not going to get sick this time.

And then comes the zinger.

worry: Are you sure?

At first, it will be hard to admit, "No, I'm not sure." It will seem like being unsure makes Worry right. That if you aren't sure, the bad thing *is* going to happen.

Still in debate mode, you might come out with a loud, "THAT ISN'T GOING TO HAPPEN."

Or get your parents to say it, "You're not going to get sick!"

Useless.

Because that kind of reassurance – the absolute guarantee kind – never works. Not if you say it, nor if you get someone to say it for you.

Absolute reassurances don't work because you know they aren't true. You can't know the future. No one can. You can't guarantee that you aren't going to get sick (any more than Worry can guarantee that you are). So the debate goes on and on.

But it doesn't have to be that way. When Worry argues: You've gotten sick before! Your stomach hurts now! You're going to get sick again!

And then clobbers you with: Are you sure?

Try this, instead:

child: Worry, you don't know what's going to happen any more than I do, but I do know this – I get stomachaches a lot, and they're usually related to you.

Or:

child: Oh Worry, give it a break. No one knows the future.

Just one strong statement. No further debate. No declaring things you don't know for sure. One statement, and that's the end of it, regardless of what Worry says next.

Try using words like, "Usually" or "Probably" or "As far as I know..." Those words are honest, and help you get used to the fact that you can't know for sure. And that that's okay.

Here are more talking back one-liners:

Oh Worry, give it a rest.

I'm not going to debate this.

I don't have a crystal ball, Worry, but neither do you.

I don't have to listen.

Things usually turn out fine.

Whatever happens, happens.

It's okay to not know.

You can think of your own one-liners ahead of time. That way you'll be prepared when Worry shows up. Because it will show up. Predictably.

If you feel anxious about trying new things, Worry will make an appearance before each new activity.

If you get nervous about looking just right, Worry will pester you as you get dressed for school.

No surprise there.

Figure out Worry's pattern, and then just *expect it.*

Instead of being all quivery as you face Worry, greet it like an old (but annoying) friend: "Hey, Worry. I was wondering when you'd show up."

If snarky is more your style: "Jeez Louise, Worry, can't you be more original?"

And if you like straightforward: "Beat it, Worry. I don't fall for your tricks anymore."

So, when you feel scared by the same thing that has scared you a hundred times before, begin to tell yourself, "That's just Worry yanking my chain."

No need for debate. No need for certainty.

Those are Worry Tricks you don't fall for anymore.

CHAPTER 8

Shifting Your Attention

So, you learn to tell Worry, "Bug off" and you refrain from debating. But Worry keeps right on talking, "Blah, blah, AWFUL THING, blah."

Should you just ignore it? *Can you* just ignore it?

Maybe. But ignoring is hard. Worry is still chattering, and there is no way to not hear it.

It's like if you were lying in bed at night and the neighbor's dog started barking. Loudly. You can't just ignore barking. The noise is everywhere.

And that barking. It's really intense. Maybe something's wrong.

Amygdala alarm!

Good thing you've been reading this book. You follow your Knows and remember that dogs bark for many reasons. Your neighbor's dog barks most nights. Most days, too. It barks at squirrels and trains and sirens and leaves. That dog is just a barker. It doesn't mean anything.

So, the barking might not mean anything, but you can still hear it. It's annoying, and hard to ignore.

Woof! Woof! Woof!

It's keeping you from doing things, like falling asleep.

Should you get up and yell at the dog?

No. That would make things worse. That dog really goes crazy when it hears yelling.

Should you lie in bed thinking about how awful it is to live next to a barking dog?

Well, you could do that. But that would be boring, and make you sad and mad. And you still wouldn't get to sleep.

What other options do you have? What should you do?

Here's what:

Acknowledge what is happening.

Observe it.

Accept it.

That's it. No grumbling. No yelling. No attempts to make it stop. Just acknowledge it, observe it, and let it be.

Acknowledge what is happening.

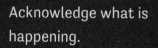

Observe it.

Accept it.

When you acknowledge an annoyance and let it be, something amazing happens. The annoying thing begins to recede. You can still hear it – Woof! Woof! Woof! – but somehow it stops being a big deal. It moves off to the side of your attention, rather than staying right at the center. It's easier, now, to focus on reading, or playing a game in your head, or relaxing to fall asleep.

Okay. Okay. That's fine for barking. But what about Worries? You can't just acknowledge, observe and accept your Worries, and let them be!

Sure you can.

The more you fight a thought or a feeling, the more it stays stuck. Center stage. Locked in place. But if you take a step back and just...observe it...it becomes less powerful, less like something you need to DO SOMETHING about.

Next time you feel worried, try acknowledging what you are thinking or feeling.

Observe and be curious about it.

Remember the things you know, still without trying to make the feeling go away.

Accept the feeling. You can do that. Just let the feeling be. No need to push it or fight it or run away from it.

Observe it. Be curious about it. Remember the truth about it. Then hang out and wait for the feeling to end.

Acknowledge what is happening.

Observe it.

Accept it.

CHAPTER 9

Hanging Out with Worry

Now you have another outsmarting Worry technique: acknowledging, observing and accepting what you are thinking and feeling, without trying to make it go away.

That's called being Mindful.

Mindfulness is a term used to describe a certain way of thinking and being in the world. Mindfulness activities help you focus on the present moment – right now – without judging that moment or leaping to conclusions about it. Mindfulness helps you feel calmer, and ultimately makes it easier to shift your attention away from troubling things, including Worries.

Mindfulness activities help you practice this way of thinking: acknowledging, observing and accepting (rather than judging, leaping to conclusions, and reacting – which is the typical mode for most of us). They do need to be practiced – every day if possible – to teach your brain to smoothly shift away from fretful Worry into this calm, accepting mode.

It works best to practice initially when you aren't worried. Then, as you get more used to being Mindful, you can start to use the techniques when you are worried, too.

There are a ton of Mindfulness activities to help you learn this way of thinking. You'll find them online or in books.

Here are two to get you started:

Follow Your Senses...

- Sit comfortably with your back straight and your arms relaxed.
- Take three slow breaths, in through your nose and out through your mouth.
- Close your eyes.
- Pick one of your senses, perhaps hearing.
- Focus on the first sound you hear. Maybe it's the fan running the heating or cooling system in whatever room you are in. Pay attention to that sound. Really listen to it. Let all the other sounds you hear fade into the background while keeping that fan noise right at the front of your awareness.
- If a thought pops into your head, notice what is happening by whispering, "thinking" or "wandering," and then let the thought go. Re-focus on the sound.
- Stay aware of the fan noise for a few minutes – telling yourself, "wandering" when you need to – then broaden your focus. Keep your eyes closed and again pay attention. What else do you hear?

- Pick another sound and zoom in on it.
- Focus on that next sound – maybe the traffic outside. Concentrate on the new sound.
- If you become aware of other noises, including the first sound you were paying attention to, simply make note of it ("fan") and then turn your attention back to the traffic.
- After a few minutes, breathe deeply and open your eyes.

Away in a Bubble...

- Sit comfortably with your back straight and arms relaxed.
- Breathe slowly and deeply three times, in through your nose and out through your mouth. As you are breathing, close your eyes.
- Think of a Worry, or some other feeling that is bothering you.
- Imagine a bubble forming around your Worry, fully enclosing it.
- Picture the bubble in your mind, clear, with just a hint of bluish tinge, like a giant soap bubble with your Worry on the inside, fully enclosed.
- In your mind, watch the bubble with your Worry inside floating away. Off into the sky. Getting smaller and smaller.

- Keep your eyes closed as you imagine the bubble drifting in the breeze, so small you can barely see it.
- Whisper goodbye to the bubble, and let it continue to float away.
- Take two more breaths and when you are ready, open your eyes.

Being Mindful helps you be less reactive to uncomfortable thoughts and feelings, including thoughts and feelings triggered by Worry. Mindfulness helps you remember that thoughts and feelings come and go, and that there is no need to debate, battle against or avoid them.

Mindfulness helps you outsmart Worry by just hanging out with it.

Look at Worry. What a fascinating creature. Jumping up and down. Making all sorts of noise.

Ho hum. Same thing over and over. Worry is predictable. Not so fascinating after all.

No need to hang out and keep watching. There are more interesting things to do.

CHAPTER 10

Worry's Biggest Trick

You are more than halfway through this book. You've learned a lot about Worry, and how to outsmart it. Let's do a quick re-cap:

★ You know you have a speedy message system between your brain and body, designed to keep you safe.

★ You know you have an amygdala that sounds an alarm – setting off the fight-or-flight response – when you are in danger.

★ You know that sometimes the alarm gets pulled by mistake, often by Worry trying to trick you.

★ You know you need to look for evidence of danger rather than jumping every time the alarm is pulled.

★ You know about recognizing and correcting Thinking Mistakes. And talking back to Worry – without getting pulled into a debate.

* You know you can't know for sure how things are going to turn out, but that being unsure is okay.
* You know you can expect Worry to show up at predictable times, so you can greet it, then tell it to take a hike.
* You know you can turn your attention away from Worry's chatter, especially if you have practiced Mindfulness.

Good for you! You are well on your way to becoming an ex-worrier. But not quite yet.

There is one more thing you need to do, and it's a biggie. You need to stop obeying your Worry.

The key to disobeying Worry is to identify – and drop – Worry-related Safety Behaviors.

Remember Safety Behaviors, from way back in Chapter 3? Safety Behaviors are the actions that arise from Danger Learning. The extra things you do – or don't do – to stay safe and feel better. You know, just in case.

Here's how it works:

DANGER ⟹ AMYGDALA ALARM ⟹ FEAR ⟹

SAFETY BEHAVIORS ⟹ RELIEF

YAY! YOU'RE SAFE

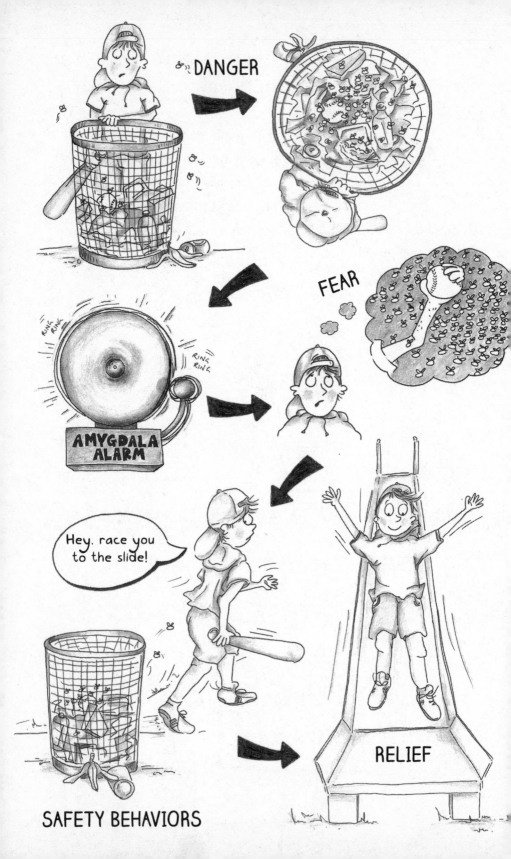

DANGER

FEAR

AMYGDALA ALARM

RING RING

RING RING

Hey, race you to the slide!

RELIEF

SAFETY BEHAVIORS

But there's also this:

PERCEPTION OF DANGER WITHOUT
ACTUAL EVIDENCE (FALSE ALARM, FOR SHORT)

⇨ AMYGDALA ALARM ⇨ FEAR

⇨ SAFETY BEHAVIORS ⇨ RELIEF

Except you were never in danger to begin with, so your fear was misplaced and your Safety Behaviors weren't necessary.
And that, Dear Reader, is Worry's biggest trick.

It mimics the pattern that happens when there is a real danger, and convinces you that your Safety Behaviors are necessary. It makes you think that you have to do them, both to stay safe and to feel better.

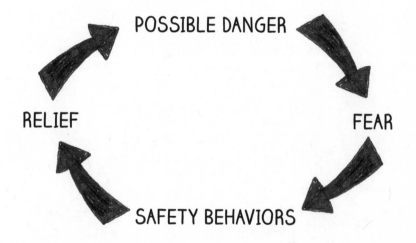

Worry traps you in a loop:

POSSIBLE DANGER

RELIEF

FEAR

SAFETY BEHAVIORS

As long as you do your Safety Behaviors, you feel better. But doing your Safety Behaviors keeps you from seeing that the Possible Danger wasn't an Actual Danger, which means your Fear was a False Alarm and the Safety Behaviors weren't necessary. Even without Safety Behaviors, you would have been okay.

It's such a clever trap. Perfectly designed to keep you in Worry's grip.

Except...

You have the key to break free.

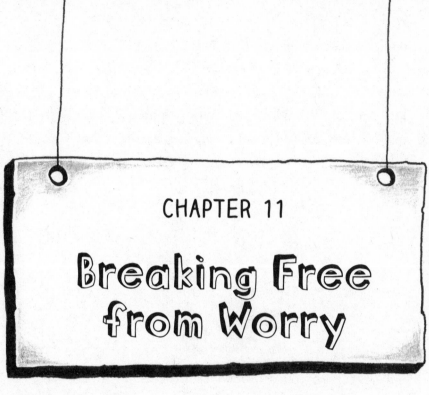

CHAPTER 11

Breaking Free from Worry

When you think you might be in danger, you do things to stay safe.

Safety Behaviors make sense when they are related to actual dangers. But they cause all sorts of problems when related to False Alarms.

Psst. Safety Behaviors.

These unnecessary Safety Behaviors take time. And energy. They grow. And can easily get out of hand.

Here's an example of how Safety Behaviors grow once Worry gets involved.

SCENARIO: Pretend you were eating a piece of chicken and it got stuck in your throat and felt – for a moment – like you might choke. Your amygdala would pull the alarm and all the information surrounding that scary episode would get stamped into your brain and be associated with DANGER.

The next time you sit down to a meal, an alarm will go off – Danger! – prompting you to take smaller bites, and chew more carefully. If you use these Safety Behaviors for just the next meal or two, and then go back to normal eating, there's no problem.

Mistake #2: Catastrophic Thinking. BIG TIME

But if Worry gets involved, watch out. Worry won't be satisfied with briefly eating cautiously. It will repeatedly whisper, "You're going to choke!"

It will tell you to adopt more extreme Safety Behaviors. And to use them, you know, forever.

Worry will push you into fight-or-flight mode every time you eat. Then, because you are on guard (your muscles are tight, your breathing is shallow), swallowing will feel odd, like you really are in danger. Worry will caution you, "Don't eat this food," "Don't eat that food," until you are down to just pasta and applesauce. Taking tiny bites. Bracing yourself every time you swallow.

That's how Safety Behaviors can start in a reasonable way, but explode into something completely unreasonable.

There are obvious problems with listening to Worry.

First, the practical stuff:

1. Eating is going to be no fun at all.
2. It's going to take forever (all that chewing).
3. You'll get sick of pasta and applesauce.
4. Your parents will never allow it.
5. Your friends will wonder "what's going on?"

But there is an even bigger problem: you are stuck in a Worry loop. Doing unnecessary Safety Behaviors. Letting Worry be the boss, and set the rules.

You need to break free. By eating chicken. Taking normal-size bites. Chewing the regular amount. Swallowing.

WORRY TRICK

 **You need to disobey Worry.**

Refuse to follow its rules.

CHAPTER 12

Jumping In

Worry wants to be the boss of you. It tries to set the rules. Rules that no one else has to follow.

Worry tells you to move away from tiny dangers. Immediately.

It makes you think you have to be sure about everything. Totally safe and totally comfortable, all the time.

Worry tells you that Safety Behaviors – like over-chewing, or avoiding, or washing, or asking for reassurance, or whatever your Safety Behaviors are – are the only way to stay safe and feel comfortable.

And then Worry tells you that you need more Safety Behaviors. And more. And more.

That's a bunch of bunk. Following an ever-expanding set of Safety Behaviors is like saying, "Yes, Oh Great Ruler," to your Worry. It's letting Worry be The Boss. Obeying makes it stronger.

The very best thing you can do is the *opposite* of what Worry is telling you.

Don't avoid scary things. Do them!

Don't move away from uncertainty. Move towards it.

Don't shy away from temporary discomfort. Embrace it.

Overblown Safety Behaviors are the problem. NOT THE SOLUTION.

Moving towards the things Worry is cautioning you about – things that make you feel uneasy or uncomfortable – is called Exposure.

Believe it or not, you already know how to do this. In fact, you do it all the time. For example:

SCENARIO: Think about going for a swim. You *know* the water is going to be cold. But you jump in anyway, despite the cold.

You Expose yourself to the water and sure enough – Brrrrrr!

Do you paddle frantically to the edge and climb out? No! You stay in and get used to it.

You "Expose" yourself to something that feels uncomfortable (in this case, cold water), on purpose, knowing you are going to get used to it. And pretty soon, you do. Within minutes of being in that cold pool, you stop noticing the cold, or being bothered by it.

The same thing happens with stinky smells, loud noises, and visiting new places. If you Expose yourself to something uncomfortable and stay put, your brain eventually stops paying attention to the uncomfortable part. You get used to it.

You already do this all the time. Now you can do it with Worries, too.

Exposure – when it comes to Worries – means stepping towards whatever Worry is cautioning you about, without using

Safety Behaviors. It means disobeying your Worry. On purpose. By doing what it is telling you not to do.

You get to control the pace.

Like the swimming pool example. There are two ways to get into a pool. Fast – just jump in. Or slow – ease yourself in a step at a time. Bracing and fast, or slow and gentle. Both work. Either is fine.

Same with Exposure to Worries. Fast or slow. Both work. Either is fine.

CHAPTER 13

Exposure

For Exposure to work, you need to Expose yourself to the right thing.

You won't get used to the cold water in a pool if you jump into a garden.

Same with Worry. You need to "jump into" the right thing.

Right things, actually – there are two.

POOL THAT WAY ⟶

When it comes to Worry, you need to Expose yourself to two things at once:

1. The situation you are avoiding.
2. The way it makes you feel.

Plug your Worry into this loop:

POSSIBLE DANGER

UNCOMFORTABLE FEELING

SAFETY BEHAVIORS

RELIEF

The loop provides the key to Exposure, helping you know what situation you are avoiding (the Possible Danger), what feeling that situation stirs up (the Uncomfortable Feeling), and what you are doing to avoid that situation (Safety Behaviors).

For example:

SCENARIO: Pretend you get stressed about your hair. It doesn't lay right, and your Worry tells you that everyone will notice, and judge you. When you brush your hair in the morning – Argh! – you get anxious and angry and stand in front of the mirror for a long time, trying to make it *right*.

IMPERFECT HAIR

RELIEF
ANXIOUS AND ANGRY

WORK ON IT FOR **40** MINUTES
LOOK AT IT FROM EVERY ANGLE
START OVER IF IT DOESN'T LOOK OR FEEL RIGHT

Exposure is always about entering a situation that makes you feel uneasy (nervous, uncomfortable, unsure) while modifying or dropping a Safety Behavior.

The first step is to plug into the loop.

The next step is to focus on your Safety Behaviors.

The third step is to think about ways to modify these Safety Behaviors, or drop them entirely.

In the case of feeling hugely stressed by your hair, here's what that last step might look like:

Safety Behavior: Wake up 40 minutes early to fix hair.
→ Exposure: Limit hair-fixing time to 30 minutes, then 20 minutes, then 10 minutes, then 5 minutes.

Safety Behavior: Check your head from every angle.
→ Exposure: Look at yourself only head-on. Eventually brush your hair without using a mirror at all.

Safety Behavior: Start over if it doesn't look or feel right.
→ Exposure: Fix hair just once. Done. No matter how it looks or feels.

Now think about how to apply this to one of your Worries.

1. Identify a Worry.
2. Plug it into the loop.
3. List the Safety Behaviors related to that Worry.
4. Figure out how to modify or drop each Safety Behavior. Remember you can do it all at once, or a step at a time.

Exposing yourself to a situation that makes you uncomfortable will trigger discomfort (fear, embarrassment, uncertainty). That's good. Well maybe not good, but useful, because the discomfort is a False Alarm and your Safety Behaviors aren't really protecting you.

Be creative. Exposure doesn't have to be tortuous. It can be goofy, too. For example:

* Crazy Hair Day (if you are stressed about getting your hair just right)
* Bee Photo Safari (if you are afraid of bees)
* Vomit Go Fish (if you are afraid of getting sick)
* Poultry Feast (if you are afraid of choking)

Even when creative, Exposure is hard work. You deserve credit for doing it. Tell yourself, *"Good job!"* each time you do an Exposure. You might also work out a reward system. Together

with your parents, create a Rewards Menu with perks and privileges for being persistent. Think of activity rewards and privileges, both of which are better than a bunch of store-bought stuff. Then give yourself a point for every Exposure you do.

Show your Worry it's not The Boss by doing Exposures in a big way. Not meekly or cringingly, but boldly. Be goofy. Be brave. Be persistent.

Repeated Exposure shrinks Worry.

CHAPTER 14

Worry in Disguise

When you read about other people's Worries, it's obvious what they need to Expose themselves to, and what they need to get used to. It's trickier trying to figure that out for yourself.

For one thing, you are in the midst of it. It's harder to see Worry from the inside.

For another, Worry is a Master of Disguise.

WORRY TRICK

Sure, some Worries are easy to recognize. They sound like this:

> what if no one talks to me?

> what if Rocko gets out when I open the door?

> what if I put my homework in the wrong place?

> what if I get sick and miss my friend's party?

Repeated questions that have to do with being laughed at or judged, with personal safety or the well-being of people you care about, are pretty obvious Worries. So are questions about things that happen the same way every day, or things you've been told and feel the need to double (and triple, and quadruple) check.

But it isn't always that easy. Worries don't always sound like Worries.

Can you spot the Worry in this sentence?

I don't want to go to baseball.

While this might sound like a child who doesn't like the sport, it's really a child afraid of messing up. How can you tell? Well, you have to listen carefully, and make guesses about the hidden message, the part that isn't exactly being said. If this sentence comes from a child who normally loves playing baseball, and typically has fun once she is there, it might just be that, "I don't want to go to baseball" really means "I don't want to go to baseball...because the players on my team are really good, and what if I strike out and everyone gets mad and thinks I'm a loser?"

Ah, there's that Worry!

But there's an even trickier part: **Worry doesn't always *feel* like Worry.**

Sometimes it feels like boredom:

> I don't WANT to walk to town. There's nothing to do. (And besides, I might get lost.)

Or personal preference:

> I don't LIKE grapes. (And besides, last year my friend got sick when he ate one.)

Or anger:

> I DON'T WANT TO GO TO BALLET! (And besides, what if you forget to pick me up when it's over?)

So, you need to look for the words beneath the words, and the feelings beneath the feelings. It's a pretty good bet that questions you ask over and over, or things you avoid that you used to like, all can be traced back to Worry.

Obvious Worry – and Worry-that-doesn't-sound-or-feel-like-Worry – both get treated the same way. Like math, remember? Same steps, no matter what the numbers.

Plug even these not-so-obvious Worries into the loop:

SITUATION ⇨ UNCOMFORTABLE FEELING

⇨ SAFETY BEHAVIORS (INCLUDING AVOIDANCE)

⇨ RELIEF

In the examples above, Safety Behaviors might include not walking to town alone, avoiding grapes, and staying home from ballet. The goal is still to practice doing the things Worry (even Worry in disguise) is telling you not to do.

Your parents can help. They know you well, and will be able to spot Worry even when it's gussied up and pretending to be something else.

You might get mad at your parents. You might be tempted to say, "I AM NOT WORRIED."

Resist that temptation. Your parents know you well, and are only trying to help.

Let them. If it's not Worry, it will be easy to do whatever they are asking you to do. If it isn't easy, chances are good it really is Worry at work.

And remember: two against one is better than one against one.

CHAPTER 15

What to Do When There Is Nothing to Do

You know that to truly break free from Worry, you need to DO things. Challenge Worry by entering new and scary situations.

WITHOUT Safety Behaviors!

But what do you do when it seems like there is no action part to Worry? Nothing to do, or not do?

Worry often comes in the form of thoughts. Thoughts that are troubling. That make you feel bad. There's nothing to do, or not do. You're just filled with these awful thoughts.

This kind of Worry thought is called an Intrusive Thought. Intrusive is related to the word 'intrude' – like an intruder, a person who comes into your house uninvited.

That's Worry all right, barging into your brain uninvited.

Intrusive Thoughts focus on things you don't want to be thinking about, things that feel horrifying. Not upsetting, like regular Worry. It's much worse than that. What's so awful about Intrusive Thoughts is that they make you feel like a bad person. And they keep repeating themselves, so it seems like it must *mean something* that you keep having the thoughts.

Intrusive Thoughts are very uncomfortable, and discomfort feels like danger, so Worry sets off the usual loop:

DANGER! ⇨ AMYGDALA ALARM ⇨ FEAR

⇨ SAFETY BEHAVIORS ⇨ RELIEF

The Danger, in this case, is the thought. The amygdala alarm is the same. The fear is obvious. And even though it might not seem like it, there are typically still Safety Behaviors designed to help you feel better.

Safety Behaviors for Intrusive Thoughts usually involve trying to avoid the thoughts, or somehow undo them.

People who have Intrusive Thoughts try to convince themselves the thoughts aren't true. They seek reassurance from others, and try not to think the thoughts, which doesn't work.

Remember: the more you fight a thought, the more it sticks.

You can use the strategies you learned in Chapters 8 and 9 when an Intrusive Thought pops into your head. Acknowledging, observing and accepting your thoughts is a form of Exposure.

You can also bring the Intrusive Thoughts to mind yourself. On purpose. Without waiting for them to come, and without using Safety Behaviors to undo them.

Psst. Mindfulness.

So even when it seems like there is nothing to do, there really is something to do. Expose yourself to the thoughts without Safety Behaviors.

SCENARIO: For example, let's say you worry about being a liar. You think about that a lot. You know lying is wrong. You don't want to be a liar. But you keep wondering if you might be lying, even a little, without realizing it.

You develop a bunch of Safety Behaviors, like starting every sentence with "I think..." That way, if what you are saying isn't totally true, at least you won't be lying because you said you weren't sure to begin with.

If you worry about lying, you will find yourself saying, "I don't know" a lot. This is a Safety

Behavior arising from suddenly feeling unsure. For example, if someone asks what your favorite flavor of ice cream is, you might think: mint chocolate chip. But then you remember eating salted caramel once and liking it. Vanilla, too. Suddenly you aren't sure what your favorite is. Naming a flavor – any flavor – feels like a lie, so you say, "I'm not sure" or "I don't know" to questions you used to just answer.

Or your mother says, "I love you," and you want to say, "I love you" back but suddenly you don't know if you do. What is love, anyway? Do you love her? Really? You were mad at your mother once. Maybe you don't love her. Do you not love your mother? You stand there, tortured by uncertainty.

Exposure – in this situation – would involve answering questions without saying, "I think" or "I don't know." It would involve making your best guess, despite your uncertainty. Talk back to your Worry, saying things like, "You're not The Boss of me" and "What I think is good enough."

You can also write down one of the thoughts (this will be surprisingly hard). Then practice saying it out loud.

You might turn the thought into a rhyme, or a rap.

Draw it in bubble letters and color them in.

When you think Intrusive Thoughts on purpose, without trying to undo them, the thoughts will eventually seem boring. Hurray! That's what you are aiming for.

You are getting used to the thought, and the way it makes you feel.

Soon, the Intrusive Thought will not seem shocking and awful.

It's just a thought. Not necessarily true. Definitely not helpful. Not so interesting after all.

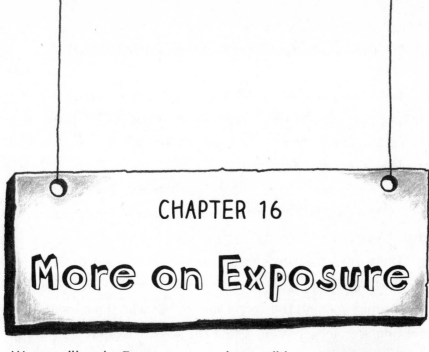

CHAPTER 16

More on Exposure

Worry will make Exposure seem impossible.
Like you aren't up to the task. That it's
too risky. Too uncomfortable.

Hopefully you no longer
fall for that Worry Trick, but
there's still this:

WORRY TRICK

Psst. That's
Thinking Mistake #3

Underestimating
YOUR ability
to cope

Why would you
even think about
Exposing yourself
to something
truly awful? Like
embarrassing
yourself in front

of everyone, or having something terrible happen to your parents?!

Keep in mind that *all* Worries are about things that seem awful. Dire possibilities you'd rather avoid. But it's not the actual bad thing you need to Expose yourself to.

That's important.

It's not the actual bad thing you need to Expose yourself to, it's the *possibility* of that bad thing. And the nervous way it makes you feel.

Think back to the chicken example. You were afraid of choking. You didn't have to make yourself choke. That would be nuts! What you had to Expose yourself to was the *possibility* of choking. Not actual choking, just the possibility of it. You had to take a chance by dropping your Safety Behaviors, and eating in a normal way.

That's the way it always goes. You don't have to make bad things happen. You just have to drop the Safety Behaviors you are using to keep them from happening.

So you can see that these Worry-related Safety Behaviors are unnecessary.

If you stick close to your parents because you are afraid something bad will happen to them, you don't have to arrange for them to get actual diseases or have tumbles off mountains! Instead, you need to practice being apart from your parents, without using Safety Behaviors.

Or let's say you get nervous talking to people you don't know well. You think people will judge you, or get angry, or laugh at you. You don't have to embarrass yourself or make people mad. You just have to stop doing the things you've been doing to prevent these things from happening.

So you'd plug into the loop and find your Safety Behaviors, and then do Exposures like:

★ Smile at a classmate you don't know well.
★ Say something at your lunch table, loud enough for everyone to hear.
★ Order for yourself in a restaurant.
★ Ask a store clerk a question.
★ Call a relative and talk to them on the phone.

SAFETY BEHAVIORS

1. Look down
2. Talk in a whisper
3. Don't greet anyone
4. Don't raise hand
5. Wait for other people to talk first
6. Get parents to ask questions

It's the fear related to the *possibility* of a bad thing that is leading to unnecessary Safety Behaviors and causing trouble.

So Exposure needs to focus on the situations that trigger that fear. Placing yourself into those situations – intentionally – without Safety Behaviors.

The more often you practice, the better.

Design several Exposures related to each Safety Behavior, to practice in multiple ways.

Once you have a list of Exposures, put it in order from easiest to hardest, or sort your list into three categories: easy, medium and hard.

And then, get started. Purposely trigger your fear. Modify or drop the Safety Behaviors you are using to protect yourself.

You are up for the challenge. Really. You can do it!

CHAPTER 17

But I'm Still Scared!

"This is hard!" you might say, "I'm still scared." If so, good for you!

Feeling scared during Exposure is a sign that you are doing it right.

Which means this is going to be hard.

It's going to feel like if you don't do your Safety Behaviors (escape, avoid, ask for reassurance, etc.), your fear will never quiet down, and you will never be okay.

SAFETY BEHAVIORS

Of course, that isn't true. But Worry tries to trick you into thinking it is. Worry pulls an alarm, which makes you feel afraid, which prompts you to do a Safety

Behavior, which pulls you into that loop of thinking you have to do the Safety Behavior to get your fear and discomfort to end.

The more you do your Safety Behaviors, the more convinced you will be that these Safety Behaviors are necessary, and the tighter Worry will have you in its grip. That's why the Safety Behaviors need to go. And they can't go without triggering fear.

It's *facing* the fear (without using Safety Behaviors) that shrinks it.

Facing the fear – really letting yourself feel it – is The Point. It is the most powerful outsmarting technique. The technique that will do the most to set you free.

That's why when you are doing Exposures, the goal is *not* to feel unafraid. The goal is to feel scared, and do the Exposure anyway. That's the only way to re-program your system, to undo incorrect Danger Learning and replace it with more accurate thinking. There isn't a way to do this without feeling fear.

Feeling scared IS THE POINT

Don't try to wipe out your fear as you are doing Exposures. Just keep your steps small (ease into the pool) so the amount of fear you feel is manageable.

If you need help with your feelings, try breathing. Breathing slowly will quiet down your amygdala (remember, that's the part of the brain that screams DANGER). Your fear won't go away entirely – that's not the point – but calm breathing might help you stick with the Exposure long enough for it to be useful.

The most relaxing way to breathe is in through your nose and out through your mouth. Make your breaths slow and deep. Concentrate on your breathing. In and out. In and out.

You can imagine a Figure Eight in your mind, or draw one on a piece of paper.

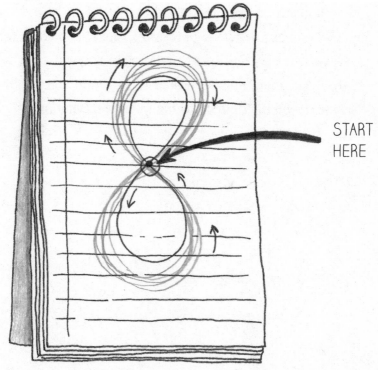

START
HERE

Start in the middle of the Eight. As you trace the top loop, breathe in slowly through your nose. When you get back to the center-point, begin to breathe out through your mouth. In... and out. In...and out.

You can count your breaths. Or repeat a word or phrase quietly to yourself. Something like "slow...down" or "I'm...okay."

If your chest feels tight – remember it might, because of the fight-or-flight response – don't worry about making your breaths deep. Just keep them slow. In...and out. In...and out.

While you breathe, coach yourself. Tell yourself, "One step... into the pool" or "False...Alarm" or "I am stronger...than my fears."

But remember, calming down isn't really the point. The point is to face your fear even though you feel afraid. To stick with the Exposure, to get used to it.

When you face your fear and Expose, Expose, Expose, your safety system will begin to do its job. You will see that you are safe, that your fear is a False Alarm. And then your fear will shrink down. Become more manageable. Disappear.

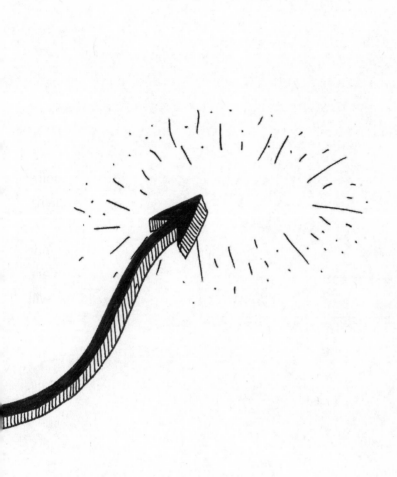

CHAPTER 18

Putting It All Together

Have you ever played an arcade game called Whack-a-Mole (also known as Splat-a-Rat)? A little plastic mole (or rat) pops up from a hole and you have to whack it to make it go down. Another little mole pops up, and you have to whack that one, too. And then another mole. And another. Each time a mole pops up anywhere on the board you have to hit it – quick – to make it go back down. Whack! Whack! Whack! And then...no more moles.

Worries are like that. Stubborn little creatures. They pop up again and again. But now you have the tools to whack them.

When a Worry pops up, whack it back down using the outsmarting techniques you have learned. When another pops up, whack that one, too.

Outsmarting Worry doesn't mean learning this stuff, doing it just once and forgetting about it. It means learning this stuff, doing it, and being prepared to use it again in the future. Over and over if need be, whenever a Worry pops up.

It doesn't matter what the Worry is about. It doesn't matter if it's an old Worry, or a new one. Whatever it is, just plug it into the techniques you have learned, like numbers in a math problem.

Re-read this book if you need to. Get the grown-ups in your life to help you: your mom, your dad, your teachers. If Worries are making things really hard, find a therapist to help, too. Use all the strategies you've learned:

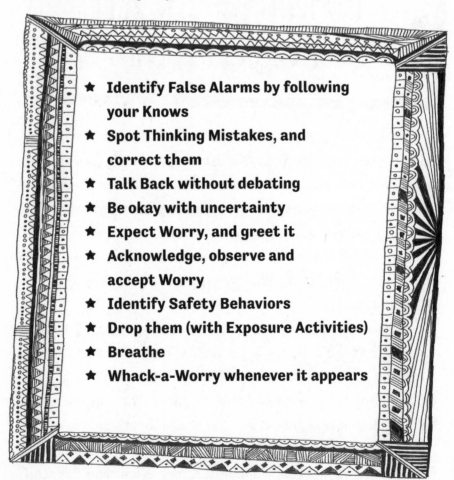

★ **Identify False Alarms by following your Knows**

★ **Spot Thinking Mistakes, and correct them**

★ **Talk Back without debating**

★ **Be okay with uncertainty**

★ **Expect Worry, and greet it**

★ **Acknowledge, observe and accept Worry**

★ **Identify Safety Behaviors**

★ **Drop them (with Exposure Activities)**

★ **Breathe**

★ **Whack-a-Worry whenever it appears**

Know these things and do these things, and feel proud of yourself. You are an expert. A person with special knowledge and skills, able to face your fears.

You are a person who outsmarts Worry.

Dawn Huebner, PhD is a Clinical Psychologist specializing in skill-building therapy for anxious children and their parents. Her award-winning self-help books for children have sold close to a million copies around the world, and have helped countless children lead happier, healthier lives. Dr Huebner is often interviewed by the media, and has given a Top-Ten TEDx talk about facing and overcoming fear. She lives and works in Exeter, NH, USA. Visit www.dawnhuebnerphd.com

Kara McHale is a graphic designer and illustrator from England. Kara has always loved to draw and paint and even won a drawing competition when she was eight years old. She studied fine art and graphic design at university and now never has to get a proper job because she gets paid to design cool things and draw pretty pictures. Visit www.karamchale.co.uk

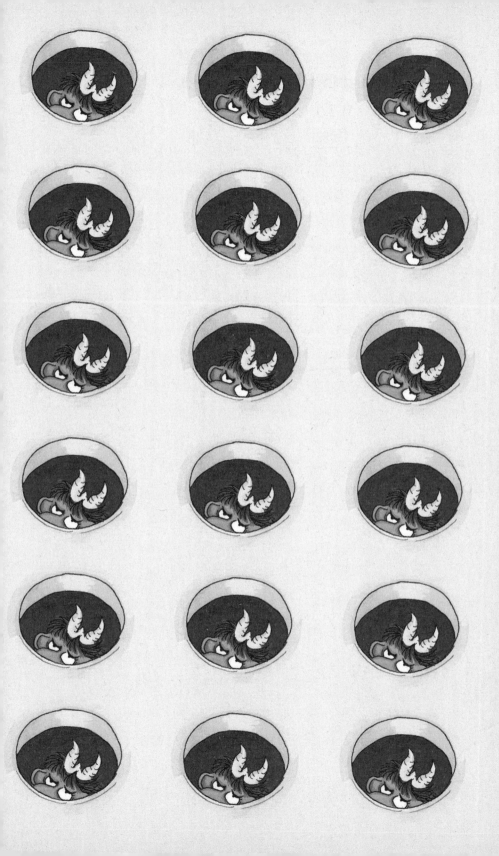

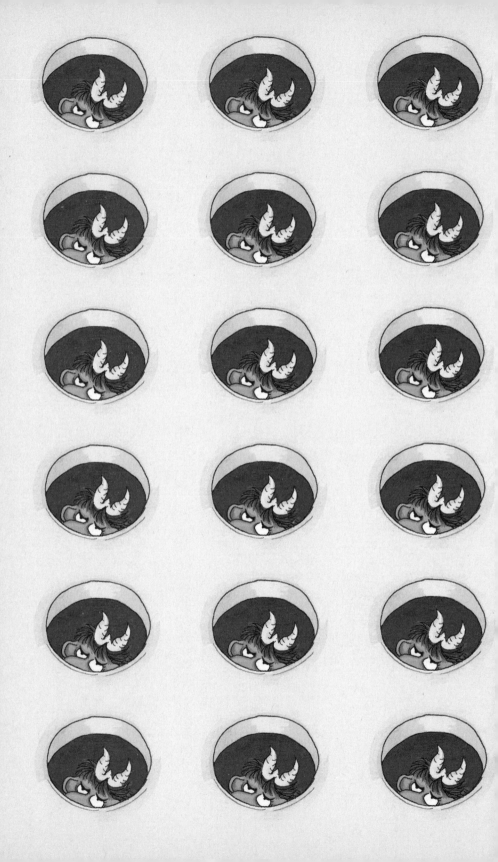